THIS MOTIVATIONAL QUOTE COLORING BOOK BELONGS TO

_____

_____

_____

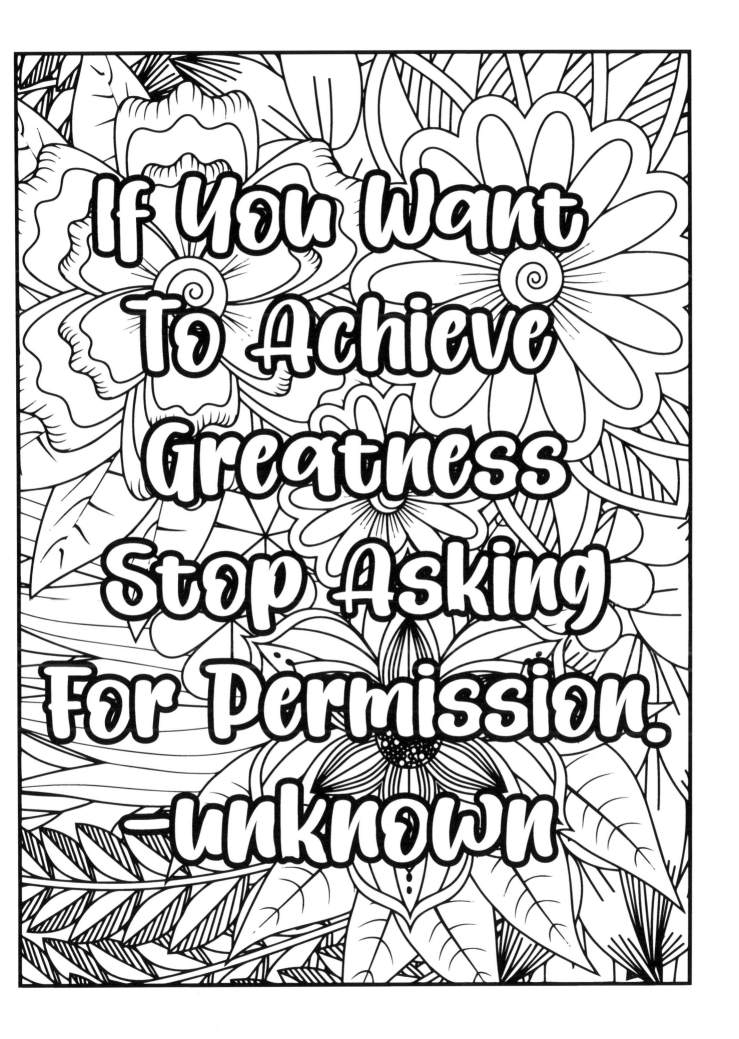

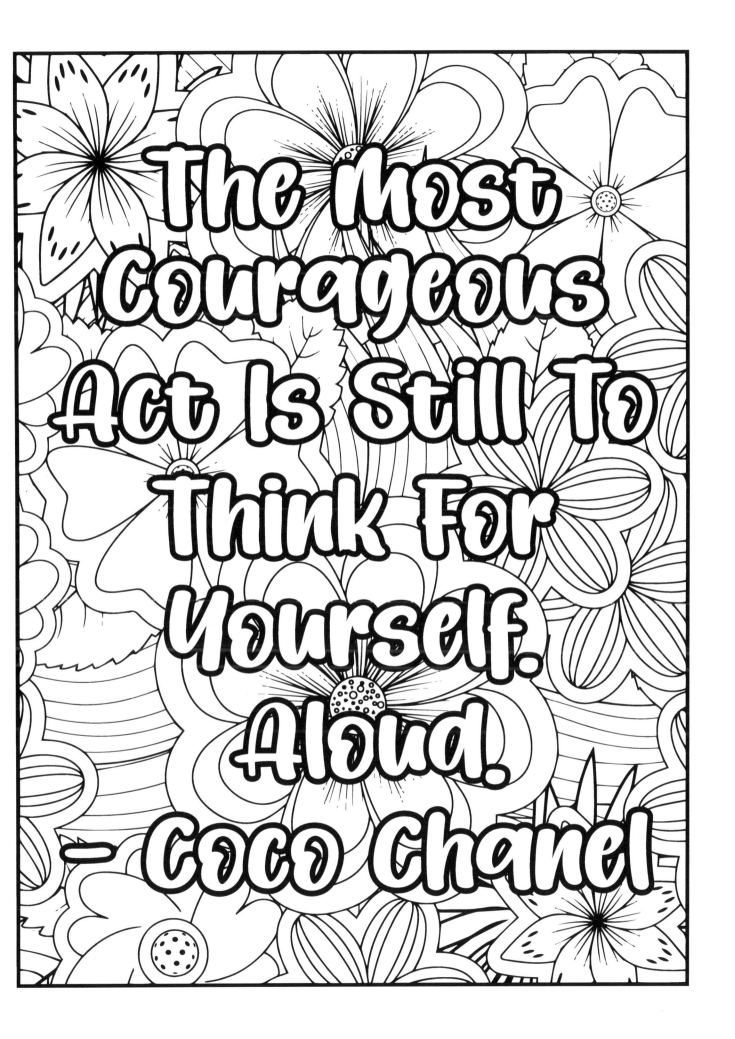

The Most Courageous Act Is Still To Think For Yourself. Aloud! -Coco Chanel

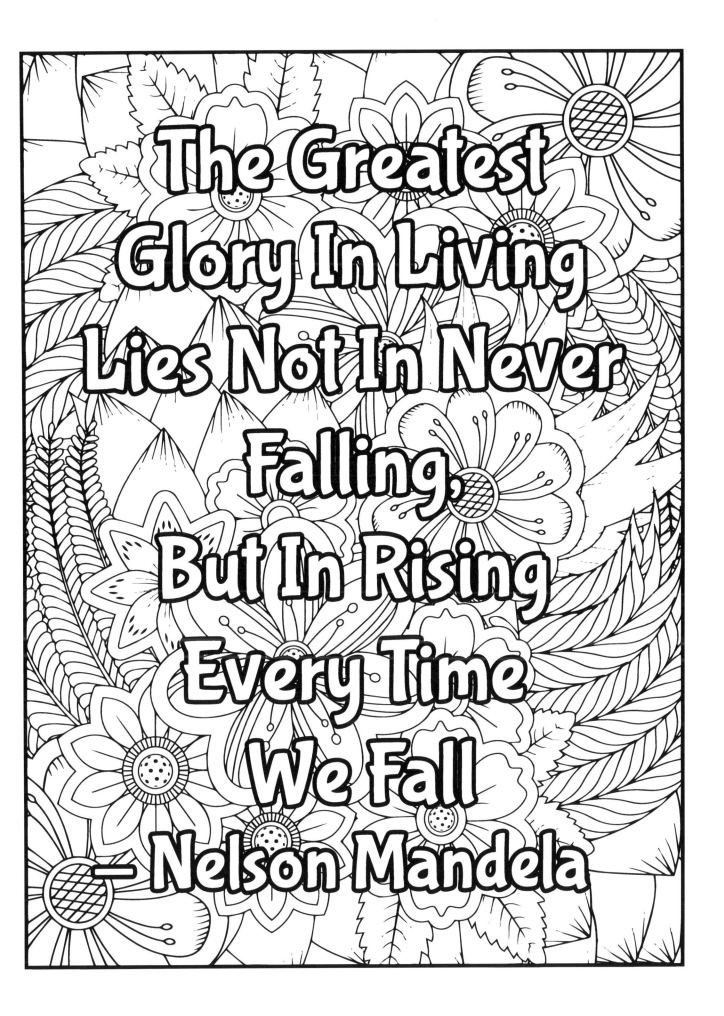

The Greatest Glory In Living Lies Not In Never Falling, But In Rising Every Time We Fall — Nelson Mandela

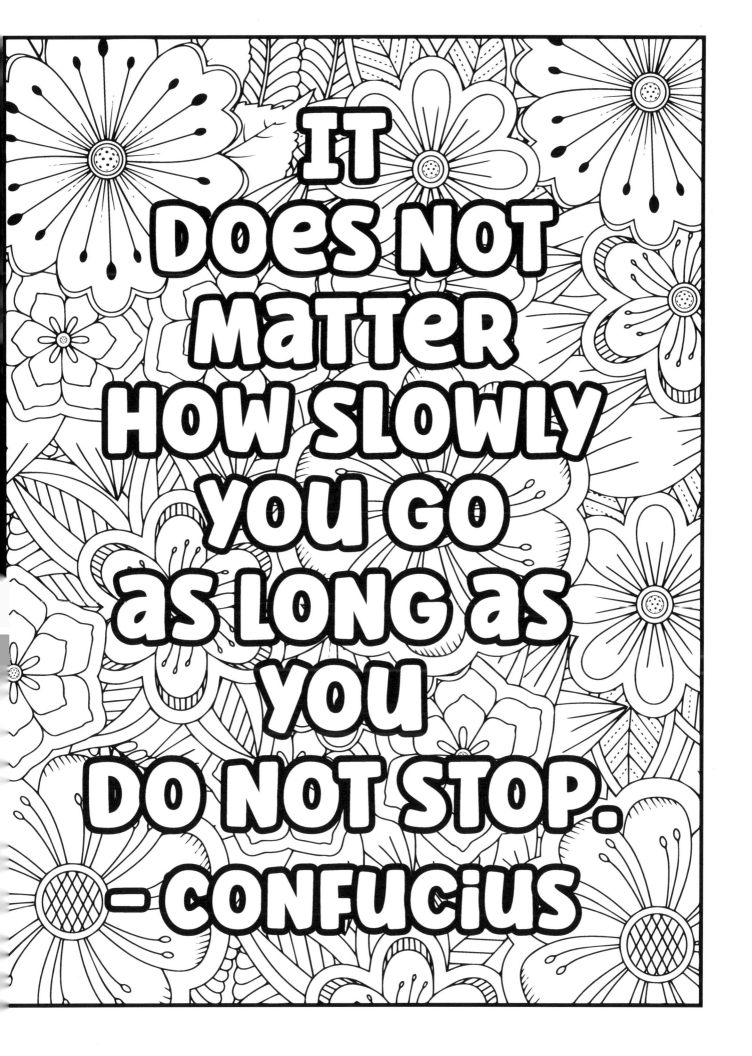

Life Is Not About Waiting For The Storm To Pass, It's About Learning How To Dance In The Rain. - Vivian Greene

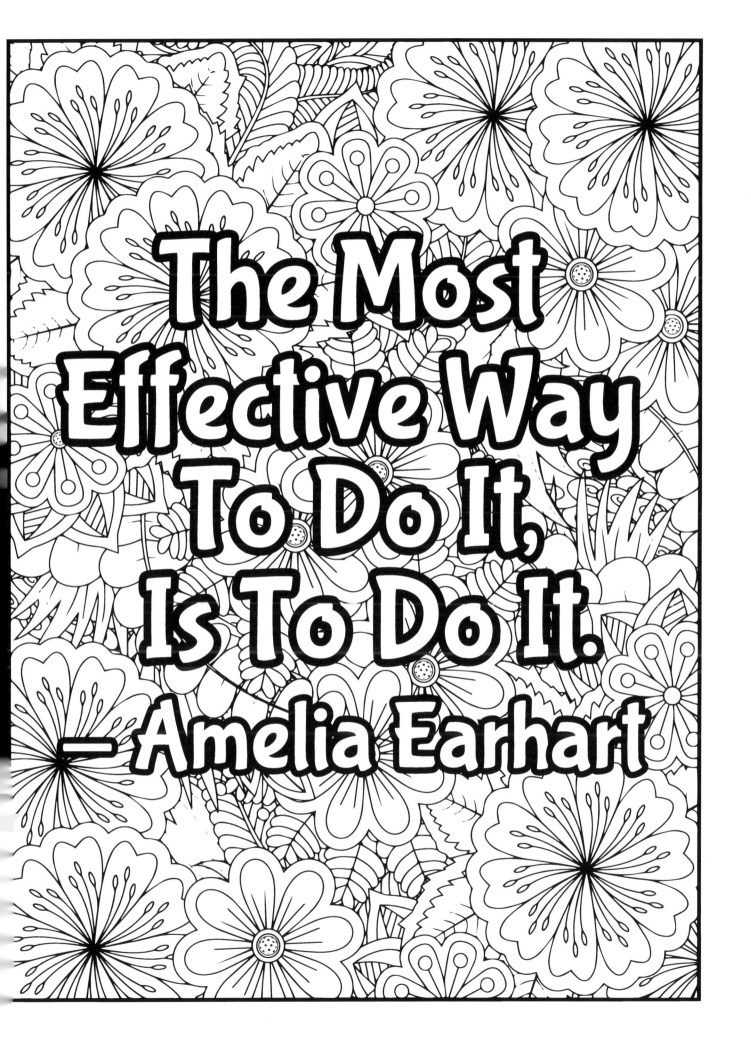

A Strong Woman
Knows
She Has
Strength Enough
For The Journey,
But A Woman Of
Strength knows
It Is In The Journey
Where
She Will
Become Strong.
-unknown

A Girl Should Be Two Things: Who And What She Wants. - Coco Chanel

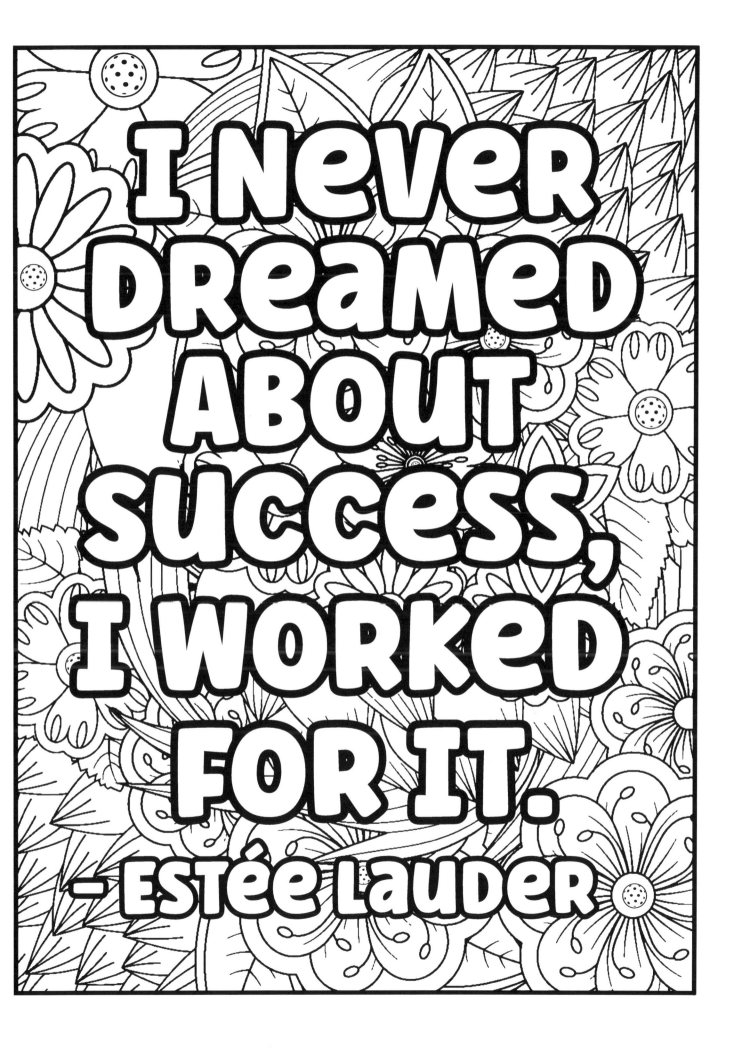

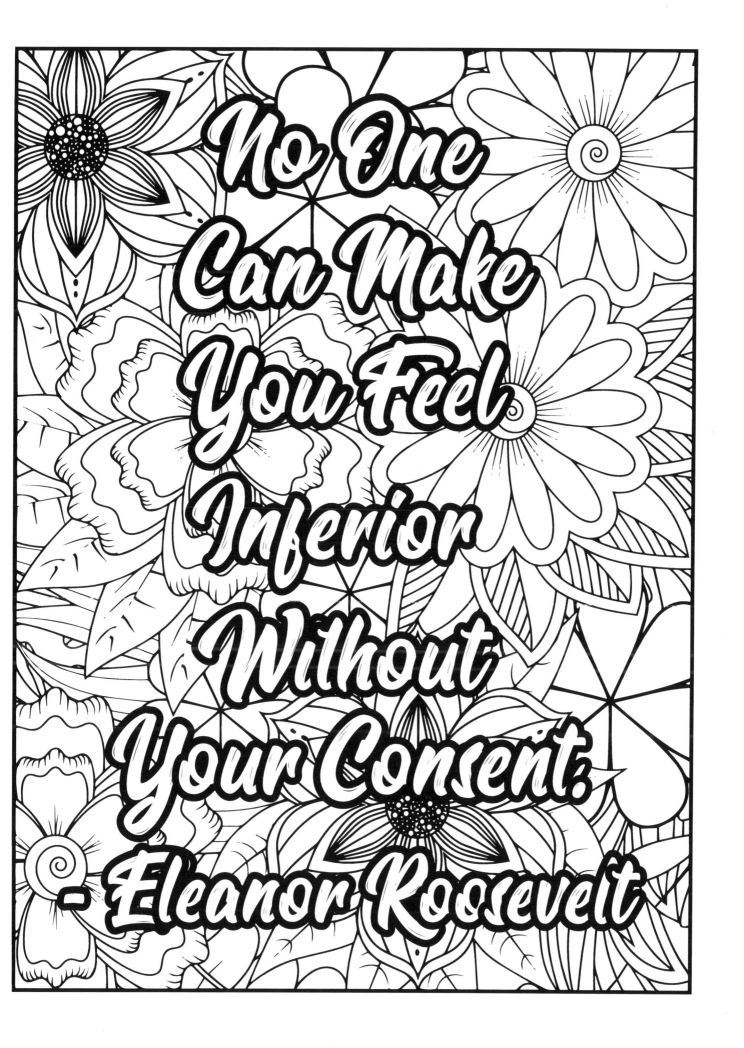

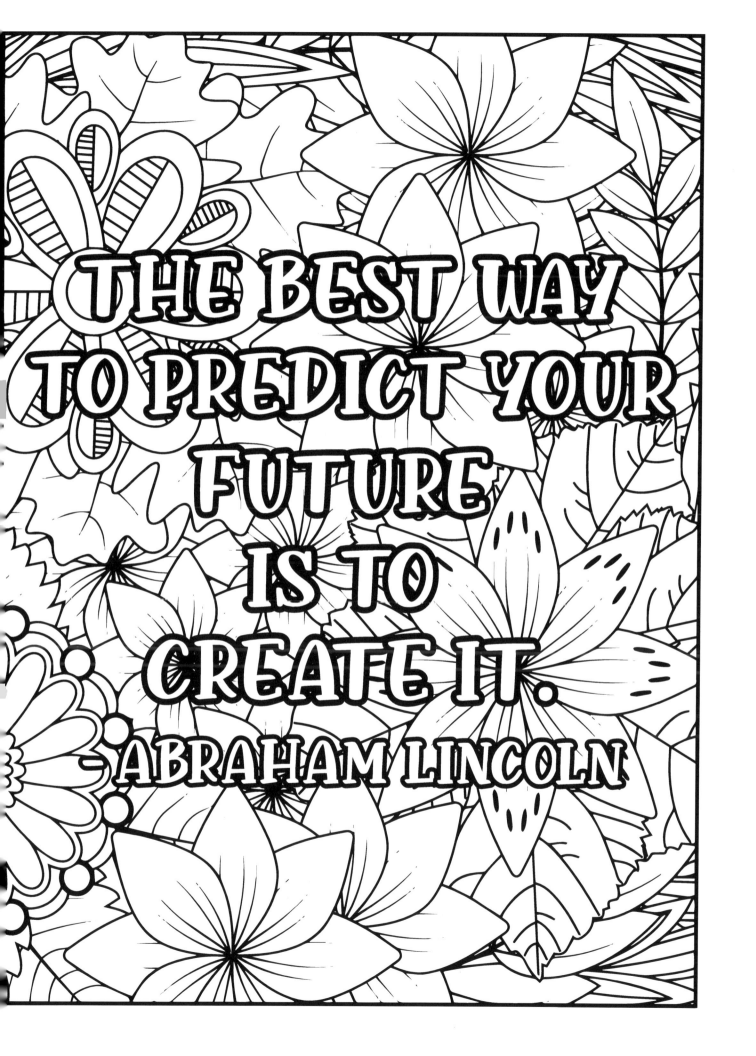

I CAN'T THINK OF ANY BETTER REPRESENTATION OF BEAUTY THAN SOMEONE WHO IS UNAFRAID TO BE HERSELF. - EMMA STONE

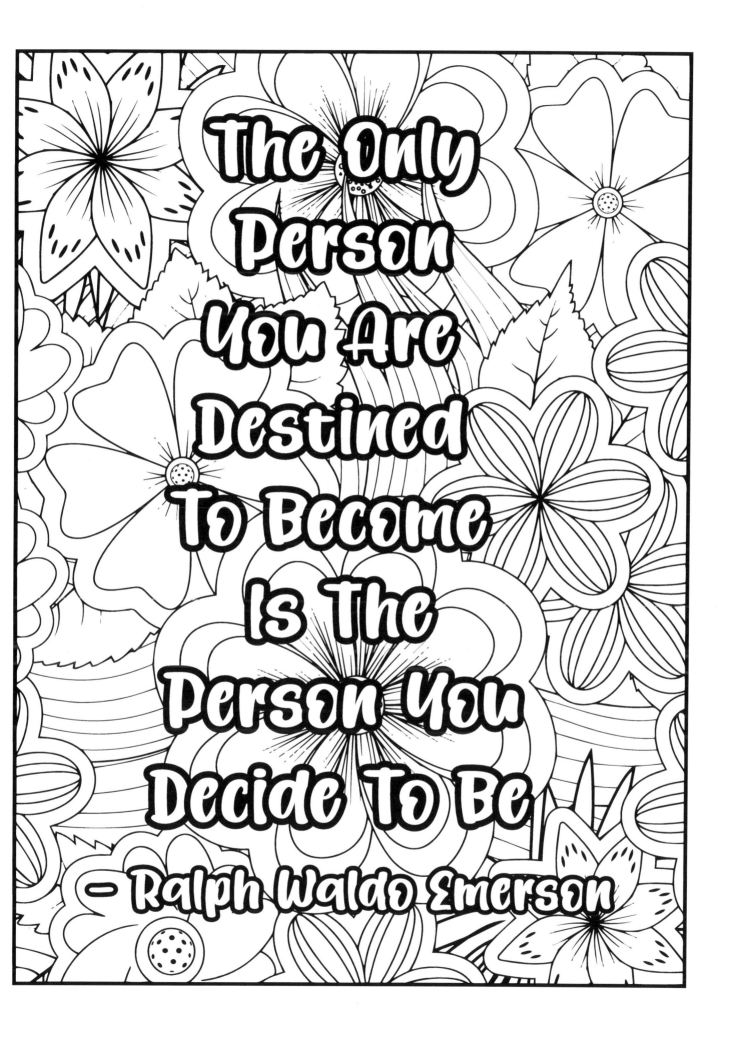

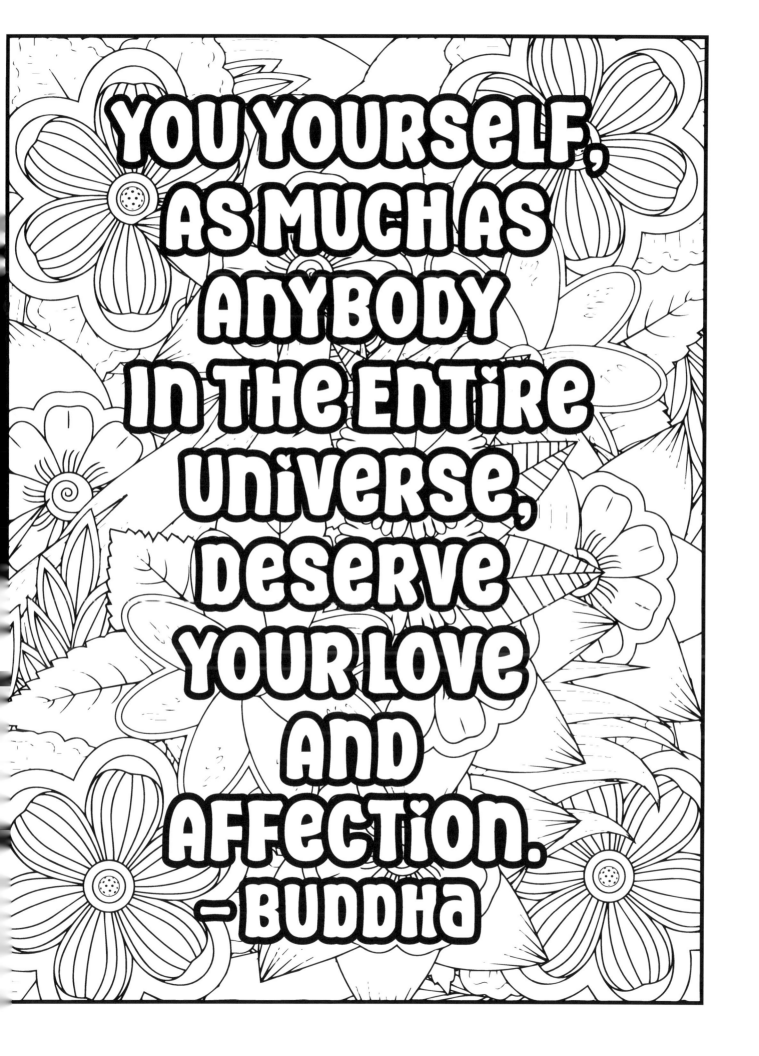

Made in the USA
Las Vegas, NV
05 November 2024

11174213R00035